EXPLORING THE WORLD OF

Foxes

Tracy C. Read

D1122165

FIREFLY BOOKS

A FIREFLY BOOK

Published by Firefly Books Ltd. 2010

3rd Printing, 2020

Publisher Cataloging-in-Publication Data
(U.S.)
Read, Tracy C.
    Foxes / Tracy C. Read.
[   ] p. : col. photos. ;   cm.
Exploring the world of.
Includes index.
ISBN: 978-1-55407-625-3 (bound)
ISBN: 978-1-55407-616-1 (pbk.)
1. Foxes - Juvenile literature.
I. Exploring the world of. II. Title.
599.74442 dc22   QL737.C22R434   2010

Library and Archives Canada
   Cataloguing in Publication
Read, Tracy C.
    Exploring the world of foxes /
  Tracy C. Read.
Includes index.
ISBN 978-1-55407-616-1 (pbk.).
ISBN 978-1-55407-625-3 (bound)
1. Foxes--Juvenile literature. I. Title
QL737.C22R42 2009
j599.775   C2009-905118-4

Published in the United States by
Firefly Books (U.S.) Inc.
P.O. Box 1338, Ellicott Station
Buffalo, New York 14205

Published in Canada by
Firefly Books Ltd.
50 Staples Avenue, Unit 1
Richmond Hill, Ontario L4B 0A7

Canadä

We acknowledge the financial support
of the Government of Canada

Cover and interior design by
Janice McLean, Bookmakers Press Inc.
jmclean14@cogeco.ca

Printed in China

CONTENTS

COOL UNDER PRESSURE

In preparation for the cold winter months, the red fox grows a thick protective coat.

MEET THE FOXES

Graceful and stealthy, curious but patient, resourceful yet adaptive, the red fox is one of nature's great success stories. Its impressive ability to make a living in a wide range of habitats, to find and capture food where less agile creatures go hungry and to raise offspring while living a largely solitary existence has earned it the reputation of a savvy survivor.

With urban development infringing on the red fox's rural habitat, even city dwellers now have a chance to spot one of these creatures up close. When I first saw the female fox that made our neighborhood her temporary territory last summer, it was an undeniable thrill. Long, lean, alert and motionless on the street cor-ner, the fox calmly turned and met my gaze, her large pointed ears and full, fluffy tail filtering the soft early-morning sunlight. A moment later, she loped lightly down the sidewalk. As she quick-ened her pace, she slunk closer to the ground, clearly on the hunt, and I understood why fox experts have dubbed this member of the dog family "the catlike canine."

Foxes are found over much of the world, yet only a few species — the red fox, arctic fox, gray fox and swift fox — make their home in North America. All share many characteristics, but none has expanded its range with the same determination as has the red fox (*Vulpes vulpes*). On planet Earth, the red fox is top dog.

4

ANATOMY LESSON

From a distance, you might mistake the red fox for a small dog. A life lived outdoors, however, tends to give the fox a lean and hungry look that sets it apart from the average pampered household pooch.

Still, as a member of the dog family, Canidae, the red fox has many doglike characteristics, from its silky reddish fur, narrow head, long, pointed muzzle and large, triangular ears to the grayish white markings on its face, throat and underbelly. The backs of its ears are black, as are its legs and paws (some say the red fox looks as though it's wearing black stockings). Its luxuriant, thick tail is flecked with black and usually tipped with white; a scent gland near the base is marked by a dark, oily patch of fur. The fox uses its long tail for balance, especially when hunting, and to signal other foxes, but the bushy tail also works as a portable wraparound heat source during cold nights on the open ground. In the summer, the fox's fur begins to fall out, or molt, and it is gradually replaced with a denser, warmer winter coat.

The male and female red fox share the same physical traits, but the male is generally a little larger. In both genders, fur color can range from yellow to a deep ruddy red and even black.

JAWS OF DEATH

Caught mid-yawn, this red fox displays its teeth and the size of its strong jaws, the better for snapping up small mammals, birds and fish.

GROWING UP FOXY

Blind and helpless at birth, fox pups weigh as little as 3½ ounces (100 g). The newborns have a short muzzle and tannish brown fur. By week two, the pups open their eyes. At nine weeks, the youngsters are starting to look more like their parents.

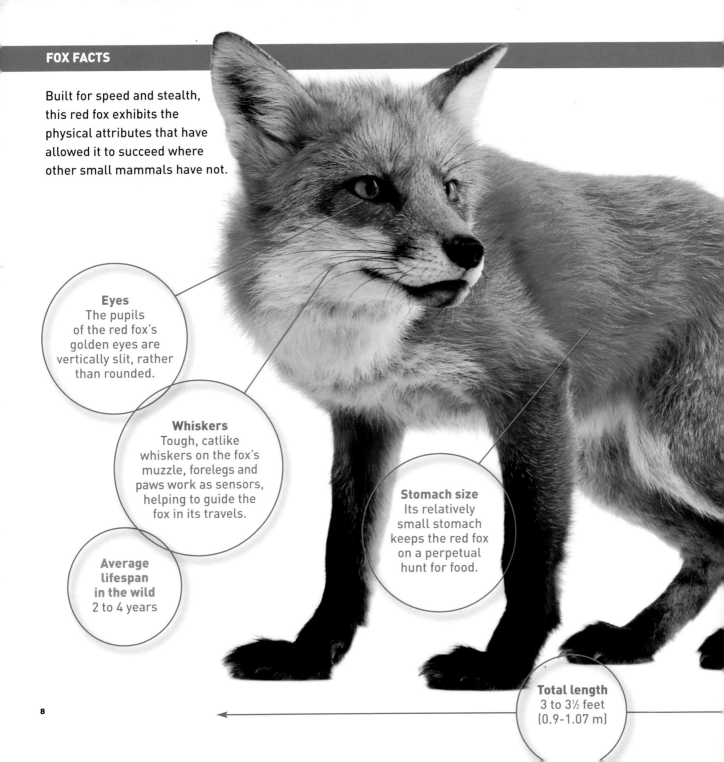

Built for speed and stealth, this red fox exhibits the physical attributes that have allowed it to succeed where other small mammals have not.

Eyes
The pupils of the red fox's golden eyes are vertically slit, rather than rounded.

Whiskers
Tough, catlike whiskers on the fox's muzzle, forelegs and paws work as sensors, helping to guide the fox in its travels.

Stomach size
Its relatively small stomach keeps the red fox on a perpetual hunt for food.

Average lifespan in the wild
2 to 4 years

Total length
3 to 3½ feet
(0.9–1.07 m)

VARIETY SHOW
The red fox species occurs in three distinct color variations: the red fox (far left) is red to rusty red; the cross fox (left) has dark markings over its back, shoulders and throat; and the silver fox (right) has black and gray fur.

Offspring
1 to 10 (typically 5 to 7) per litter; 1 litter per year

Special features
Long hind legs allow the red fox to jump up to 7 feet (2.1 m) into the air from a standing position.

Tail
Ranging from 13½ to 16½ inches (34-42 cm) long, the red fox's bushy tail usually has a white tip. (A dark, oily patch of fur near the base indicates the presence of a scent gland.)

Weight
The male and female are fairly close in size, weighing in at 8 to 15 pounds (3.6-6.8 kg) and up to 30 pounds (13.6 kg).

Fox on the run
The red fox has been clocked at 30 miles per hour (48 kph). Its lightweight build contributes to its speed and agility.

NATURAL TALENTS

The fox counts on every one of its five senses — sight, hearing, smell, taste and touch — to be the best hunter it can be.

With its vertically slit pupils, which are common to cats, not dogs (whose pupils are rounded), the fox is able to narrow its focus and distinguish moving shapes in different kinds of light. And that's an asset for this primarily dusk-to-dawn hunter, one that may be especially helpful for spotting prey at ground level.

Perched back on its head, the red fox's large ears funnel sound messages about the location of the fox's next meal. The rustle of a mouse under dry autumn leaves, the buzz of an insect on a spring evening and the muffled movement of a rabbit or hare can all be detected by the fox's highly tuned hearing.

Its excellent hearing keeps the fox informed about nearby predators as well and enables the canid to stay in touch with other foxes by picking up the high-pitched vocalizations they use to communicate, from doglike barks, shrieks and whines to growls, screams and coughs.

Its long muzzle and relatively large nose indicate that smell is another important sense. Smell can lead the fox to bird nests and rabbit burrows, as well as animal carcasses. It also helps the fox keep track of the caches of food it has hidden away throughout its territory.

SURVIVAL GEAR
With its large funnel-like ears, sharp eyes and sensitive nose, this red fox is on the alert.

While the fox is skilled at picking up the scent of prey, it also marks its territory with a powerful scent recognizable to other foxes and even humans. At the same time, to avoid detection, it sometimes disguises all trace of its presence by rolling in rank-smelling feces or decaying flesh.

The red fox's wide-ranging sense of taste is central to both its survival and its success. With taste buds that respond favorably to everything from small mammals and rotting roadkill to insects, fruits and nuts, the omnivorous red fox can make a meal out of almost anything.

All mammals are covered with hair, but some, like members of the dog and cat families, have specialized hairs called whiskers. The fox's whiskers occur on the muzzle, the forelegs and even the pads of its paws. Studies suggest that the whiskers enable the fox to gather information about its surroundings through touch and help guide the fox as it moves through its territory.

RED ALERT
This prey fell victim to the red fox's sharp eyesight, finely tuned hearing and lightning-quick reflexes.

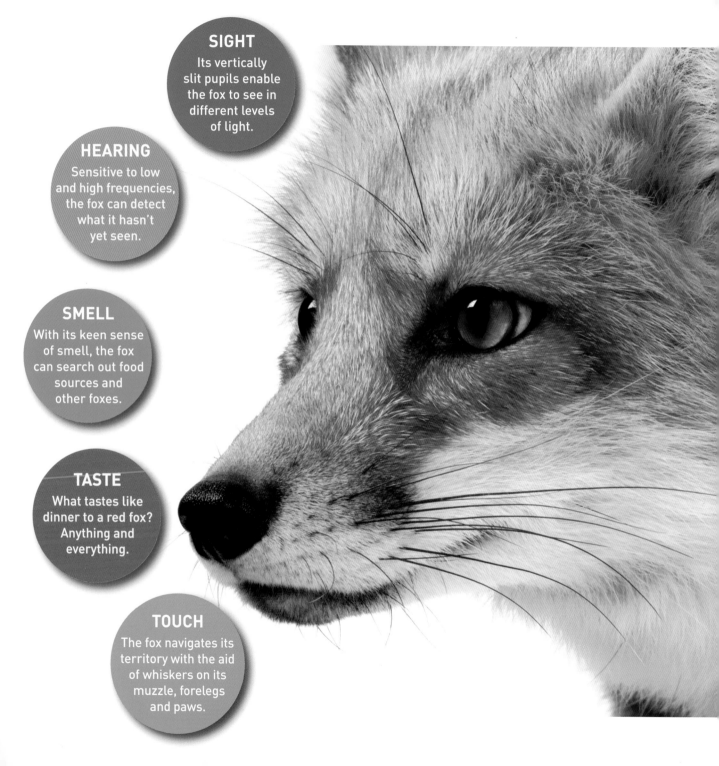

SIGHT
Its vertically slit pupils enable the fox to see in different levels of light.

HEARING
Sensitive to low and high frequencies, the fox can detect what it hasn't yet seen.

SMELL
With its keen sense of smell, the fox can search out food sources and other foxes.

TASTE
What tastes like dinner to a red fox? Anything and everything.

TOUCH
The fox navigates its territory with the aid of whiskers on its muzzle, forelegs and paws.

HUNTING FOR SUCCESS

In order to survive, all animals need a place to live and reliable food and water supplies. Some animals are restricted to very specific diets, and those diets, in turn, dictate where they can live. But the healthy red fox populations across much of the United States and in all of Canada, as well as in the United Kingdom, Europe, Asia, northern Africa and southern Australia (where the fox was introduced for hunting in the late 19th century), demonstrate that the red fox is able to thrive in a wide range of environments. What's the secret of its success?

For starters, the red fox is an omnivore — it can and will eat virtually anything and everything, depending on what is available from season to season. It is also a superb hunter and succeeds in catching much of its targeted prey, from tiny rodents, like voles and mice, to small mammals, such as squirrels and rabbits.

Like many other animals, the fox stashes food in hiding places known as caches, to be uncovered and eaten when the hunting is poor. It can also get by on fruits, nuts, grasses and other plants. In this way, the fox has been able to adapt to life in a variety of landscapes, from prairies, grasslands, meadows, mixed forest and farmland to the frozen Arctic tundra. Recently, as cities expand and take over the fox's traditional rural territories, it has even started to settle in urban neighborhoods,

WORKING HARD FOR A LIVING

When stalking prey, the red fox moves from a crouch to a "slink run," followed by a low jump, jaws ready to grasp its victim. The fox has been known to lunge 25 feet (7.6 m) downhill in pursuit of a small rodent.

The most successful wild carnivore worldwide, the red fox has staked a claim in the United Kingdom, Europe, Asia, Africa and Australia. It is also found in much of the central and eastern United States and in every province and territory in Canada.

where there is ready access to rodents, backyard garden produce and the occasional small pet.

Through observing the red fox in the field, scientists have learned a lot about its hunting techniques. A solitary creature that is most active from dusk to dawn, the fox hunts small animals it can capture and kill on its own, unlike the wolf, which hunts in packs, taking down and sharing much larger prey. One advantage of solo stalking is that it allows the fox to use the element of surprise. When spying a vole in a field, the fox silently sneaks up on it, careful to avoid making any noise that would alert its prey. Then it crouches low and springs into the air, dropping on its victim in a dramatic downward lunge. If all goes as planned, the vole is trapped under the fox's front paws, to be eaten or cached.

A slightly different hunting style is used with birds and tree squirrels. Moving from a crouch into a "slink run," the fox makes a low jump and attempts to grab the prey in its jaws.

When chasing a fast-moving rabbit, the fox uses a more conventional high-speed method, while its approach to insect or worm hunting is less intense, which may tell us something about where these meals rate on the fox's list of favorite treats. But whatever the hunting strategy, the red fox continues to prove that it has what it takes to survive.

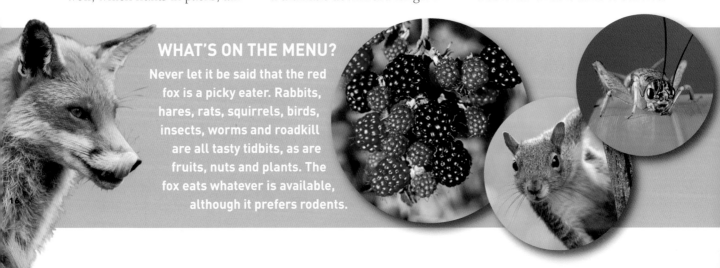

WHAT'S ON THE MENU?

Never let it be said that the red fox is a picky eater. Rabbits, hares, rats, squirrels, birds, insects, worms and roadkill are all tasty tidbits, as are fruits, nuts and plants. The fox eats whatever is available, although it prefers rodents.

PLAY & LEARN

For fox pups, playtime is all about fine-tuning the skills they will rely on as adults. This high-flying youngster is working on its hunting pounce.

PLAYING HOUSE

The harsh, unearthly sound of a red fox barking on a cold, clear winter night often means one thing: It's mating season.

A fox is able to communicate with other foxes by leaving scent messages around its territory using urine and glandular secretions, much as domestic dogs do. During the late fall, these messages increase and their pungent smell gets stronger. In this way, the male fox is signaling that he's ready to find a mate. That signal is reinforced with increased vocalizations, often between two or more males competing for a female.

Once a male and a vixen meet, they go through a short courtship period, getting to know each other. In early spring, less than two months after they mate, their litter — typically five to seven pups, also called kits or cubs — is born.

By then, the vixen has found a safe place to give birth and raise the pups. She is fairly flexible about the den location. What's most important is that the den is warm and secure. Some vixens dig a hollow along a stream bank, at the edge of a woods or under a barn or shed; others take over the abandoned burrow of a woodchuck or badger.

The main entrance often faces the sunny south. The den sometimes has emergency exits, and the vixen may even set up alternate dens, where the pups can be taken if danger threatens. Dens may be used again the following

MEET & GREET

Affectionate grooming and play between a male and a female are part of the courtship ritual.

year, but in the winter, the red fox sleeps out in the open.

Fox pups are totally dependent on their mother for the first few weeks. During that time, the male's job is to bring food to the vixen and protect the family. After a month or so, the pups venture outdoors, and the parents begin to share the duties of pup rearing. Through playful interactions with one another and their parents, the pups start to learn valuable life skills, such as how to recognize the smell of prey and how to stalk a vole or a mouse.

The pups are weaned at two months of age. By then, their baby blue eyes have turned golden and the camouflage color of their first coat is starting to redden. Soon, they start going out on short hunting trips with their parents.

At six months, the pups are fully grown, and the family unit usually separates, although female pups may stay on longer. By winter, the young foxes are ready to start their own families.

SIBLING RIVALRY

From an early age, fox pups fight for power in the family hierarchy, often viciously.

HOME SWEET DEN

Until the age of two months, fox pups stick close to the den.

MEET THE NEIGHBORS

There are many species and subspecies of fox in the world, but only four make their home in North America. The red fox is one, and its three continental cousins are worth noting.

The arctic fox (*Alopex lagopus*) lives in the Far North. Its summer fur is dark brown and yellow-white, while in winter, it boasts a plush white coat that keeps it warm and provides camouflage against the snow. A carnivore, the arctic fox hunts small land and marine mammals, using its keen sense of smell and acute hearing to locate prey under the snow.

The gray fox (*Urocyon cinereoargenteus*) normally avoids the open farmland that the red fox has made its own, preferring hilly terrain and wooded areas ranging from southern Ontario to Venezuela. About the size of the red fox, the gray fox has a thicker coat that is reddish on its chest and belly and grizzled on its back and tail. One of its outstanding characteristics is the ability to climb trees; it sometimes even nests high up in a hollow tree.

The compact buff-and-gray-colored swift fox (*Vulpes velox*) roams the shortgrass prairie and desert, hunting jackrabbits, birds and insects with the speed its name implies. In the 1930s, Canadian farmers mistook this canid for a livestock predator and almost poisoned the swift fox population out of existence. Today, it is making a comeback.

LOCATION, LOCATION, LOCATION

Although their territories may overlap that of the red fox, the swift fox (top left), gray fox (bottom left) and cold-hardy arctic fox (left) have specific preferences in their choice of habitat.